ALPHABET SONGS

Starring: Melody

Table of Contents

Cast of Characters

Songwriters: Wendy Wiseman & Sari Dajani
Melody: Wendy Wiseman
Rhythm: Sari Dajani
Singers: Wendy Wiseman, Sari Dajani, Jasmine Arbour, Al Di Buono, Timothe Gendron
Musicians: Sari Dajani, Wendy Wiseman

Educational Activities:
Jennifer Jesse, Mike Drebenstedt
Graphic Design & Illustration:
Jennifer Jesse, Neal Rasmussen, Cindy Rasmussen

Any Questions? 1-888-321-KIDS

Come visit our Award Winning Website: www.kidzup.com

Alphabet Fun

A _____	B _____
C _____	D _____
E _____	F _____
G _____	H _____
I _____	J _____
K _____	L _____
M _____	N _____
O _____	P _____
Q _____	R _____
S _____	T _____
U _____	V _____
W _____	X _____
Y _____	Z _____

Name an animal, an object or a cartoon character
that begins with each letter of the alphabet.

ABC Color Matching

Giraffe

Cabbage

Ball A

Lady Bug

Bubble

Fairy

Match and color each group of letters:

G = Green	A = Orange	C = Dark Blue	Y = Black
I = Yellow	F = Purple	L = Pink	B = Red
R = Light Blue	E = Brown	D = Gray	U = Hot Pink

Write Your ABC's

Aa Bb Cc Dd Ee Ff Gg

Hh Ii Jj Kk Ll Mm Nn

Oo Pp Qq Rr Ss Tt Uu

Vv Ww Xx Yy Zz

Practice writing the Uppercase and Lowercase Alphabet.

Mystery Letter

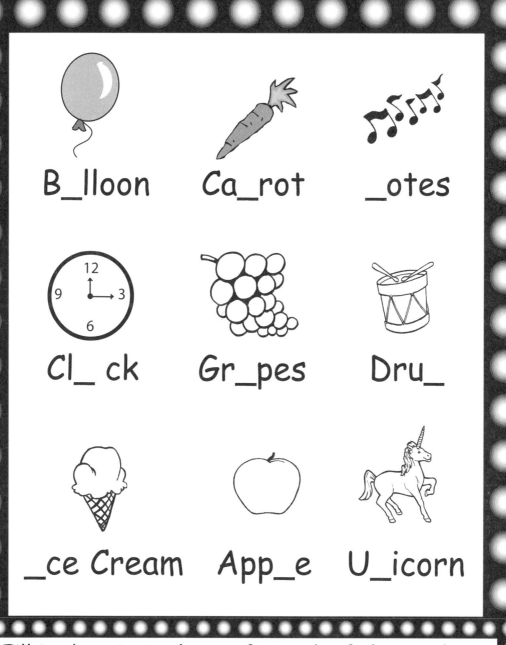

B_lloon   Ca_rot   _otes

Cl_ ck   Gr_pes   Dru_

_ce Cream   App_e   U_icorn

Fill in the missing letter for each of the words.

Letter Match

_emon

_iolin

_icket

_abbit

T
M
G
I
D
L
A
V
R
F

_ish

_rum

_rapes

_asks

Draw a line to match the first letter of each object's name.

Word Search

```
C O I N T E R A Z Y
X L M J F A O L P B
Y K L O L L I P O P
O A P P L E R E A M
G G Z D A G N R P K
U R W C D R I N K L
R A A M R S A B N H
T P J E B N R F I E
Z E L N U X N U T S
F S X A N S L E T J
```

1. Coin
2. Yogurt
3. Nuts
4. Lollipop
5. Drink
6. Apple
7. Grapes
8. Bun

All the words listed above appear in the puzzle.
Find them and CIRCLE THEIR LETTERS ONLY.

Hi I'm **A**
And I'm here today
To introduce you
To the **Alphabet** Play

A is for **actor**
Just like me
I'm the **announcer**
With **allergies (atchoo)**

A is for **apples**
And apricots
For **answers** to questions
You **ask a** lot

A is for **animals**
Alligators and ants
Aardvarks and apes
And alley cats

Always remember
A starts the fun
Now the **Alphabet** Play
Has begun

B is here
With a **big bang boom**
You'd **better believe** it
Or leave the room

Baseballs, basketballs,
And **bats** and **brooms**
Busy bees buzzing
Beside the **baboon**

Brown and **black**
Beige and **blue**
Bubbles and **bobbles**
And **bright balloons**

Bushes and **bushels**
Of flowers in **bloom**
Bye-bye for now
Be back soon

8

Curly Cue C
Yes that's me
I'm **coy** and I am **cute**
And I am **cuddly**

My cousin **Candy**
Has a real **cool cat**
He drinks **coffee** with **cream**
From his **custom**-made **cap**

Cabbage, **carrots** and **celery**
Add **cauliflower**
And **create** a soup for me

I've **completed** my **caper**
I'm leaving with grace
The **clock** is ticking
And D is on my **case**!

Ding dong ding dong
Who is there?
The letter D
Dashing and **debonair**

He is making his **debut**
In a **dramatic** way
He's **dreaming** of **directing**
The rest of the **day**

The **dogs** and the **ducks**
Decide to **delay**
The **daisies** and **daffodils**
Went on their way

D is **departing**
As the **drama** unfolds
And E's in the wings
So let the **drums** roll

9

E is **entertaining**
And **enters** with **ease**
So **enthusiastic** and
Eager to please
E is **everywhere**
E is a part of the team
E is a vowel
Held in high **esteem**

Elks and **eels**
Emus and **elephants**
Eggs and **enchiladas**
Endives and **eggplants**

As **E exits**
The **end** is very near
This **episode** is over
Now F can appear

Flamboyant F
With **fiery** hair
Has a **furious** temper
But is **fancy** and **fair**

F is no **fool**
She's always cool
With lots of **flair**

F can be **funny**
Friendly or **formal**
F can be **frantic**
Frivolous
Or normal!

F is a **fox**
A **flower** or a **frog**
F is a **fish**
A **fly** in the **fog**

Fire fighters
Farmers and **fiddlers**
All love **F**
Don't you?

10

G is for **Gordy**
He is from **Germany**
A **generous gentleman**
He enters **gallantly**

Gesturing to a **gang**
Of **grasshoppers** and **geese**
Gorillas and **giraffes**
On their way to **Greece**

He **gazes** at **gardens**
As he **gallops** along
Geraniums, gardenias
Greet him with a song

G is **getting** ready
He's **going** to the **gate**
'Cause H is hollering
"Hurry up I'm late!"

H isn't rude
She's **hyper** that's all
Humming to **herself**
Hurrying down the **hall**

"**Hi** everybody!
Hope I'm not late
I'm **happy** to be **here**
So **hip hip hooray**!
Hundreds of **hamsters**
Are saying **hello**
Hyenas and **hippos**
Put on a show

H isn't **hasty**
She's got a big **heart**
Here's a **huge hug**
It's time to depart

I've got an **idea**
I think is **ideal**
It is so **impressive**
An **incredible** deal

It improves every **instant**
It's increasing in size
It's instinctively inspiring
Do you realize?

Oh how **interesting it is**
To **invent** such a thought
This **is intriguing**
Is it not?

I haven't any clue
This **is** so **ironic**
I can't remember my **idea**
But **I'm** not going to panic!

Jazzy J
Is a **joker** you see
He's a **jolly** old **jester**
Just wonderful to me

On his **jaunt** to the **jungle**
He met **Jack** and **Jill**
They were **jumping joyfully**
Jogging down the hill
Jazzy J is a **joker** you see

On the **journey J** met **John**
And **Judy** from **Japan**
Who gave him **jellybeans**
And a **jar** of **jam**

Now **J** got a **job**
In a **jumbo jet**
Flying to **Jamaica**
With a **jaguar** pet
Jazzy J is a **joker,** you see

The **king** of **koalas**
Kookaburra is here
Kindly kissing everybody
Who dares to come near

Knock knock who's there?
It is **K kangaroo**
The **karate** expert
And **kung-fu** too

Three little **kittens**
Are playing **kazoo**
Eating shish **kebabs**
And **kiwis**
With **kids** in the zoo

K is **knitting knee** socks
K is **kneading** dough
L is putting on her **knapsack**
Let's go!

L is a **lady**
Who **laughs** a **lot**
Loves lettuce and **lemons**
And **leeks** and shallots

She **looks like** a **leader**
A **legend** of all times
She's **loyal, level**-headed
Loves limericks and rhymes

Leaping lizards are **lurking**
As **lions lay** by
The **llamas** and **lynx**
Are **looking** at the sky

The **lights** are **low**
L has to **leave**
M has arrived
With magic up his sleeve

13

In order to know the **nature** of **N**
You **need** to know about him
He's **neither** a **nag** nor **naive**
He's **neat** and uses a **napkin**

He **nibbles** his **noodles**
With his **nephew Ned**
Next to his **niece Nadine**
At **night** before they go to sleep
They eat **nutritious nectarines**

He has a **noisy neighbor**
Who **naps** in the afternoon
He **never neglects** to watch the **news**
In his white and **navy-blue** room

Nelly the **nurse** is a **nice** person
Who always **nurtured N**
She's been his **nanny** all his life
And will be till the end

M the **magnificent magician**
Merrily marches in
In a **manner** so **majestic**
It **makes** you want to grin

He also loves to **mimic**
He's a **master** at it too
He **masquerades** at
Mardi-Gras
Mysteriously he **moves**
His **music** is a **masterpiece**
Of rhythm and **melody**
And **many** have been **mesmerized**
By his wizardry

M's minute is over
Let's **mosey** on by
We're in the **middle**
Of the alphabet
My how time flies!

14

If you **observe** the letter O
It's **obvious** you'll see
Its round like an **orbit**,
Or oval in shape
As easy to draw as can be

A wise **old owl** named **Ozzie**
Once overheard the **ox**
Say to the **oyster** and **octopus**
To hide the **ostrich** in the box

At 7 **o'clock**, by the **old oak** tree
The **orchestra** will play
An **original organ** and **oboe** recital
Oh, what a beautiful day!

In my most humble **opinion**
I think the letter O
Is **on** it's way **out**
Get ready, get set, let's go!

P **parades** with **panache**
She has a **perfect pace**
Her **personality** is **pleasing**
She has a **pretty** face

She has a **poodle** and a **parrot**
A **pig** and a **panda** too
P has **plenty** of **pets**
And these are just a few

Pass the **plate** of **pumpkin pie**
The bowls of **porridge please**
Don't forget the bread **pudding**
The **potatoes** and the **peas**

Prepare to **put** your PJ's on
It's time for bed and **prayers**
Q is waiting **patiently**
At the top of the stairs

Q is almost always
Followed by a U
Q is shaped like an O
With a line running through

Q is **quiet**
Q is **quick**
Without a **question**
Q is slick

Q is **quality**
Q won't **quit**
Just the opposite
Yes, just the opposite

The **quails** are **queuing**
The **queen** will depart
Quack quack said the duck
There's the letter R

Rudolf the **red** nose **reindeer**
Got his name from letter **R**
Running around the **roof** tops
He can **really ride** so far

Robert the **rabbit raced** him
It was **rapidly** pouring **rain**
Ray the **raccoon** was humming
Such a beautiful **refrain**

Down the **road** there is a **river**
Right beside the **robin's** nest
Can you hear nature's **rhythm**
Makes me **relax** and **rest**
I hear the sleigh bells **ringing**
Announcing the time to **return**
R is getting **restless**
It's now S's turn
Rudolf the **red** nose **reindeer**
Got his name from letter **R**

Tom the **T** is a **teacher** you can **trust**
A **talented teller** of **tales**
Tom can **tackle** any **topic**
He's as **tough** as nails

Tom has a **tendency to talk too** much
And **trips** over his feet
When it's **time** for Halloween
He will **trick** or **treat**

Now take a **seat** and **sit** down
See what S can do
She's shaped like a **snake**
She's skinny as a rake
She will **sing** a **song** or two

Now **Terry the tiger travels**
In **trucks, tractors,**
Trailers and **tankers**
On **Tuesday** he wears his
Turquoise T-shirts
And **tees** off with
Teddy the banker.

Her **soft** voice can **soothe** you to **sleep**
Sounds she makes are **sweet**
So special she is
She's smart as a whiz
She is **strong** and **savvy** and neat

Tina the turtle
drinks **tea** from a **teacup**
Has **terrific table** manners **too**
She likes **turkey** on **toast**
With **tomatoes** on **top**
And says "**Ta-ta**" when she is **through**

In **summer she** likes to
See-saw and **slide**
And **swing** and hide and **seek**
She's so surprising
And **sensitive** too
S is **surely** unique

U looks **unique** in his **uniform**
He's an **undercover** cop
He **uses** his mind to **unravel** mysteries
He's **undeniably** the cream of the crop

My **uncle** runs **uphill**
Kite **under** his arm
Up, up, up and away it flies
Through the **universe upside** down
The **ultimate** flying machine in the skies

U is easy to **use** any time
And that's **unquestionablely** true
I'm getting **undressed**
And I'm sure you've guessed
The letter V is coming through

The letter **V** gets my **vote**
He has a **valid** point of **view**
V is a **valuable** letter
And **very versatile** too

On his **vacation** he took a **voyage**
To a **valley** with a beautiful **view**
The colors were **vivid**,
The nature was **vibrant**
A **vision** of beauty too

If you know your **vocabulary**
And if you know your **verbs**
If you stick two **V's** together
W will start the words!

18

"Welcome" waves W
To the **walrus walking** by
Where is the **wolf**,
I **wonder**?
What, when and **why**?

The **whale** in the **water**
Watching the **weathervane**
Worried about the **wind**
And **warnings** of heavy rain

Wait a minute!
Who are you?
The letter **W**
That's **who**!

There aren't many
words in the alphabet
That start with **X** or **Y** or **Z**
But we will try to find a few
No matter how hard it may be

For **X** there is **X-ray**
And **xylophone**
I can't think of many more
Now find your own!

Y has a few more words
Like **yarn** and **yawn** and **yes**
These are the ones
That come to mind the best

Z is the last letter
That **zooms** it's way around
Zebras, zoos, zippers, zigzags
And has a **zany** sound

We're at the end
We're almost done
Learning the alphabet
Is so much fun

Time to say good-bye
We're done for today
This is the end
Of the Alphabet Play!
Bye-Bye!

Name That Snack!

Cheese

Melon

Carrot

Grapes

Apple

Banana

Ice Cream

Draw a line to match the snack's name with it's picture.

Letter Search

PACMLO

Find the letters in Melody's face and color them:

P = Green	A = Orange	C = Dark Blue
M = Yellow	L = Purple	O = Pink

Word Search

```
L E A V E S T O R X
O F J U A Z B Y C W
F D V I E U F T G S
L S E A S O N S T R
O H Q E I P C R W S
W N J B S N O W I P
E K F A L L E N N R
R A Z B Y M G A T I
S U M M E R N S E N
S U N S H I N E R G
```

1. Winter   4. Summer   7. Fall
2. Snow   5. Seasons   8. Sunshine
3. Flowers   6. Spring   9. Leaves

All the words listed above appear in the puzzle.
Find them and CIRCLE THEIR LETTERS ONLY.

Letter Maze

Help Melody find her way to the exit!

23

Crossword Puzzle

Write the words in the appropriate space.
Giraffe, Elephant, Camel, Monkey, Zebra, Gecko